Are You Full of S.H.I.T.

(Senseless, Harmful, Intrusive Thoughts)?

Are You Full of S.H.I.T.
(Senseless, Harmful, Intrusive Thoughts)?

Go from Crappy to Happy

GINA E. MCGUIRE

BALBOA.
PRESS
A DIVISION OF HAY HOUSE

Balboa Press books may be ordered through booksellers or by contacting:

Balboa Press
A Division of Hay House
1663 Liberty Drive
Bloomington, IN 47403
www.balboapress.com
1-(877) 407-4847

Because of the dynamic nature of the Internet, any web addresses or links contained in this book may have changed since publication and may no longer be valid. The views expressed in this work are solely those of the author and do not necessarily reflect the views of the publisher, and the publisher hereby disclaims any responsibility for them.

The author of this book does not dispense medical advice or prescribe the use of any technique as a form of treatment for physical, emotional, or medical problems without the advice of a physician, either directly or indirectly. The intent of the author is only to offer information of a general nature to help you in your quest for emotional and spiritual well-being. In the event you use any of the information in this book for yourself, which is your constitutional right, the author and the publisher assume no responsibility for your actions.

Any people depicted in stock imagery provided by Thinkstock are models, and such images are being used for illustrative purposes only.
Certain stock imagery © Thinkstock.

Printed in the United States of America.

ISBN: 978-1-4525-7812-5 (sc)
ISBN: 978-1-4525-7814-9 (hc)
ISBN: 978-1-4525-7813-2 (e)

Library of Congress Control Number: 2013913032

Balboa Press rev. date: 08/14/2013

Congratulations!

●●

You've made the decision to flush out senseless, harmful, intrusive thoughts from your mind. The simple act of wiping away negative thought patterns will transform you from crappy to happy as you learn to potty train your brain.

You may choose to read this book straight through from beginning to end. You may decide to choose a topic that's specific to what you're experiencing at the present time. You can find advice that will help guide you through the holiday season. Or you may even decide to trust the wisdom of the universe, open the book to any random page, and see what message lies there.

The secret to change is repetition. Your brain grows on what you feed it. Keep this little book handy; read and reread the concepts while you're trying to clean up your act. Even though you may have an occasional "accident," your brain will learn to change itself over time. Happiness is just a thought or two away.

Take a load off your mind!

Gina

Table of Contents

. . . .

Pessimism

No pessimist ever discovered the secret of the stars or
sailed an uncharted land, or opened a new doorway for
the human spirit.

—Helen Keller

Have you become an Eeyore? "Lost my tail. Gonna rain."
What great things did a pessimist ever accomplish?

Maybe you're suffering from a case of the Too Bads:
*I'm too old, too tired, too busy, too short, too fat. I've got a
bad back, bad knees, bad attitude, bad luck, bad breath.*

It's high time to stop listening to the Itty Bitty Pity
Committee inside your head. Cancel out every self-
imposed limitation and self-sabotaging thought.
Replace the Too Bads with the Four Ups:

1. Get up.
2. Dress up
3. Show up.
4. Look up.

Engaging in positive thinking over time will physically create new neural pathways in your brain. It's like rewiring your brain for success. Negative thoughts will always pass by the doorway to your mind, but you don't need to invite them in and entertain them for a while. Just let them walk on by.

Helen Keller lost her hearing and vision at eighteen months of age. Against all odds, she went on to graduate from Radcliffe College, earn honorary doctoral degrees from Temple University and Harvard University, and receive accolades and awards too numerous to mention. She was an accomplished writer and speaker, an advocate for the disabled, and a philanthropist. She died at age eighty-seven. In her eulogy, she was fondly remembered as a woman who showed the world there are no boundaries to courage and faith.

Put away your umbrella. Here comes the sun.

Rain, rain, go away!

Age

• •

> How old would you be if you didn't know how old
> you were?
>
> —Satchel Paige

Too often, we limit ourselves by how we think someone of our age should act or dress. We accept that the best time to do a certain thing is dictated solely by age, by some mythical time that we are waiting for or somehow missed and can never recapture.

It has been said that aging is a privilege denied to many. You're here now, and as I am fond of saying, you're going to be dead for a long time. Why not make the most of wherever you are in your life's journey and stop limiting yourself to a number?

George Burns won his first Oscar at age eighty. Golda Meir was seventy-one when she became prime minister of Israel. Albert Schweitzer was still performing surgery in his African hospital at age eighty-nine.

How old do you think they felt?

Change

3

. . . .

> Grant me the serenity to accept the people I cannot change, the courage to change the one I can, and the wisdom to know it's me.
>
> —Author unknown

The new serenity prayer above reminds us that the only people who really like others to change them are wet babies.

It's easier to blame someone else when things go wrong, far easier than taking a fearless moral inventory of our own shortcomings. We're certain that everyone would be better off if they only listened to us. But if you spend too much time focusing on everyone else's problems, you may be avoiding looking at your own. Be clear with yourself about the one thing you can control—how you want to live *your* one precious life.

Personal change starts with a *you*-turn in perspective. Let everyone else find their own way, unless they need a diaper change!

Go, baby!

Positive Energy

4

· ·

There are two types of people in the world: those who brighten a room when they walk in and those who brighten a room when they walk out.

—Bill Sanders

Which one are you?

Have you ever entered a room and immediately felt the negative energy? Dealing with angry and disgruntled people on a regular basis can impact not only your mental health but your physical health as well. These energy vampires leave you feeling emotionally drained, tense, and exhausted.

Repeated exposure to negative people can lead to depression and physical illness. Keep in mind that no one can make you feel bad or inferior without your consent. Take nothing personally. Strive to light up the room. When you do, your health improves and the energy vampires lose their power.

Whether it's positive or negative, your energy has a ripple effect. Do a little housekeeping. Leave the room in a better place than you found it.

Vampires suck.

Originality

. . . .

Be yourself. Everyone else is already taken.

—Oscar Wilde

Warning: You are an endangered species!

There will never again, in the history of all the world, be another person exactly like you. Remember when your mother said, "They really broke the mold when they made you"? She was right. If you are spending even one moment comparing yourself to anyone else, you are wasting your time.

Look around at all of nature. Trees don't try to be flowers. Cats don't try to be dogs. They are what they are. Even inside your own body, your liver isn't pouting about not being your stomach. It's not envious of the spleen or grumbling about how the pancreas has it made. It's just doing the unique job it was created for, and so should you.

You are a special edition, never to be reissued. There is something that only you can offer the world, in a way that no one has ever offered it before or ever will again. Instead of fretting about why the grass isn't greener on your side, start by taking better care of your own extraordinary lawn.

On your mark. Get set. Mow!

6

Freedom

. . . .

The chains which cramp us most are those which weigh
on us least.

Sophie Swetchine

Many of us spend time wringing our hands over the
way things used to be or the way things should be. "If
only they'd do something about . . ." we say, or, "I'll
be happy when . . . ."

Have you settled into a life of complacency,
unconsciously giving your power away? Are you
waiting for a cosmic sign to set you free? There is
nothing external that's going to fulfill you. If you are
not happy with who you are now, it's unlikely that
winning the lottery or meeting your soul mate is going
to change that. If there's a situation that's concerning
you, take action. To quote the Hopi elders, "We are
the ones for whom we have been waiting."

We forge our own chains with the thoughts we think.
We open the door to personal freedom by changing our
internal dialogue. The most important conversation

you will have today is the one you have with yourself. Say nothing to yourself that you wouldn't say to your best friend. Don't live under lock and key.

Unchain your heart.

Kindness

7

∙∙∙∙∙∙∙∙∙∙∙∙∙∙∙∙∙∙∙∙∙∙∙∙∙∙∙∙∙∙

> If you were arrested for acts of kindness, would there
> be enough evidence to convict you?
>
> —Author unknown

Even if you're not a runner, you've probably heard
of that blissful feeling called the "runner's high" that
comes after a strenuous workout. But did you know
that there is such a thing as a "helper's high"?

Studies have been conducted on volunteers from
across the country, and all reported a rush of euphoria
immediately following an act of kindness, which leads
to a prolonged period of improved emotional well-
being. This state of bliss is triggered by the release
of endorphins, the body's natural pain reliever that
is responsible for both the runner's and the helper's
highs.

Better yet, both the giver and receiver of those acts
experience an increase in serotonin, a neurotransmitter
that acts like a happy drug to elevate mood. Believe it
or not, the giver of the kind act actually experiences

a greater increase in this happy drug. Apparently it is better to give than to receive after all!

What a profound difference there would be in the world if each of us tried a little tenderness. It wouldn't be a trial, and the change would be arresting!

Thanksgiving

8

. . . .

If the only prayer you ever say in your whole life is "thank you," that would suffice.

—Meister Eckhart

Thanksgiving isn't just a holiday, it's also a verb. Have you said "thank you" today?

Were you thankful just to wake up today? Have you considered the alternative? Be grateful for another day, another chance, a clean slate.

Did you have something to eat today? One-third of the world's population is starving. Another third is underfed.

Do you have clean drinking water? Billions of people around the globe die annually from drinking contaminated water.

Did you sleep in a bed last night? If so, consider yourself more fortunate than the one hundred million homeless people worldwide.

And if you're reading this right now, you are not only alive, but you can read. One billion people in the world are illiterate.

Tomorrow morning when you open your eyes, before you even get out of bed, be thankful for waking up. Be thankful for another new day. Your whole life will change when you start with an attitude of gratitude.

But why wait until tomorrow?

Happy thanks-giving!

Gossip

9

· ·

I've always believed that a lot of the troubles in the world would disappear if we were talking to each other instead of about each other.

—Ronald Reagan

Welcome to the Drama-Free Zone. It's where we secretly gossip about someone's virtues and attributes behind their backs. Wouldn't the world be a great place if this were true?

Gossip—we've all done it. Sadly, gossip seems to be part of the human condition. We're bombarded with scandalous headlines while we wait in line to pay for our groceries. We're titillated by claims from outrageous sound bites before upcoming news broadcasts. Television series are based solely upon airing the dirty laundry of celebrities.

Negativity is contagious, and gossip spreads like wildfire. It has been said that those who gossip *with* you will gossip *about* you, so beware of passing on a piece of sensationalism about another human being. It just may be your fifteen minutes of fame one day.

Try an experiment in your life. Every time you are within earshot of gossip, make it your mission to change the subject. Mention a positive quality about the person in question. Talk about the weather, a new recipe, a sports team . . . anything but another human being. We have far more in common than we realize. We all have the same basic needs, and no one needs gossip to survive.

If gossip is human nature's telephone, are you willing to hang up?

10

Christmas Season

· ·

If I am not for myself, who will be for me? And if I am
only for myself, what am I? And if not now, when?
—Rabbi Hillel the Elder

Lesson number one is to look out for Number One.
There's no line of people waiting to make sure that
you take care of yourself. No one is going to check
if you flossed your teeth or ate your vegetables today.
But remember that self-care includes not only your
*p*hysical needs but your *m*ental and *s*piritual needs as
well. Think of it as having PMS. Care for all of you,
because you're all you've got!

Lesson number two is to look out for others. Do
you remember which gifts you got for Christmas five
years ago? If you get an iPhone 27 this year, it will be
obsolete by next year. But if you've donated time at a
soup kitchen or adopted a needy family for Christmas,
would you remember that? Kindness is contagious,
and that's the one thing we should all catch at the
holidays and all year through.

Lesson number three is that there's no better time than now, because now is all there is. The past is over, and no one is promised the future. Your life is happening right now, and this is not a dress rehearsal. Why wait until January to start your resolutions? What are you waiting for?

Who? You. When? Now.

Resolve to evolve.

Taking Control

11

. . . .

The bad news is time flies. The good news is you're the pilot.

—Michael Altshuler

Are you scared to fly—to actually physically board a plane and leave terra firma? Be thankful you weren't doing so in the 1930s. The following instructions are from one of the first manuals for flight attendants:

- Keep the clock and altimeter wound up.
- Carry a railroad timetable in case the plane is grounded.
- Warn the passengers against throwing their cigars and cigarettes out the windows.
- Keep an eye on passengers when they go to the lavatory to be sure they don't mistakenly go out the emergency exit.

We certainly have come a long way.

But perhaps you're grounded on the tarmac of life, never cleared for takeoff. Who is behind the wheel of your plane?

Maybe you haven't left the ground because you're afraid of what other people will think. But are you living your life for you or for other people? If the opinions of your neighbors are what matters most to you, then stay the course. If you are not being true to yourself because it might disappoint your friends or coworkers, then who's actually in the cockpit?

You can pilot your plane or sit back in coach. It's time to fly the friendly skies.

Up, up, and away!

Christmas Season

12

· ·

Isn't there anyone who knows what Christmas is all about?

—Charlie Brown

Yes, indeed, Charlie Brown, there certainly is someone who knows.

Maybe you're not in the Christmas spirit this year. Perhaps you've spent some time bellyaching to others who share your lack of interest in this holiday. It's possible that you perceive it as a major inconvenience and expense and, quite frankly, just not worth the bother. Bah, humbug.

Meet the Grinch. Of all the unlikely characters, he knows the true meaning of Christmas. But he learned it only after a considerable amount of complaining, scheming, and plotting to stop a holiday that just cannot be stopped. He worked as deviously and diligently as he could (accompanied only by his happy little dog, Max) at ruining any chance that the Whos down in Whoville would celebrate Christmas. It came anyway.

What he discovered should be our mantra for this Christmas and every one to follow:

Then the Grinch thought of something he hadn't before. What if Christmas, he thought, doesn't come from a store. What if Christmas, perhaps, means a little bit more?

The Whos agreed wholeheartedly. They sang in unison, without presents or even a speck of food, "Christmas time is in our grasp, as long as we have hands to clasp."

Calvin Coolidge once said that Christmas is not a time or a season, but a state of mind. Perhaps he originally came from Whoville.

May Christmas live in your hearts and minds all year long, and may you always have a hand to clasp.

New Year's Resolutions

13

. . . .

> We will open the book. Its pages are blank. We are
> going to put words on them ourselves. The book is
> called Opportunity and its first chapter is New Year's
> Day.
>
> —Edith Lovejoy Pierce

You know the drill. It happens every December when you review all the promises you made to yourself last year. You were going to lose weight, start a regular exercise program, spend less money, be a better parent, partner, person—all while advancing your degree, buying a new house, and writing a book. No pressure there.

When the truth sets in, you start to admonish yourself for being a failure. How did another year go by? Why did so many of these goals remain unmet once again?

What is wrong with me?

The lesson and legacy of the previous year is a simple one: If you are not happy now, it's unlikely that an advanced degree or ten pounds less on the scale is going to be the tipping point. It's equally unlikely that January first will hold all of the willpower and empathy that you were lacking twenty-four hours earlier.

But you can start today to let go of unrealistic expectations. Maybe you're trying to live up to an ideal that you imagine other people have of you. It is oftentimes just as courageous to let go of something as it is to hang on to it. What perceptions do you have that no longer serve you? Maybe it's time to turn off the pressure cooker.

Why not make your New Year's resolution a simple and powerful one: *I will be a happier and more grateful person this year.* So simple, it just might work!

Don't let another resolution go in one year and out the other.

14

Making Decisions

• •

Insanity: doing the same thing over and over again and
expecting different results.

—Albert Einstein

Webster's Dictionary defines *insanity* as a "deranged
state of mind," but I like the definition attributed to
Einstein better, because at one time or another, we are
all a little bit insane.

Is there a problem or situation in your life that keeps
going around and around like a broken record? Do
you find yourself reacting the same way over and over
again to a certain person or issue? Einstein tells us that
we can't solve a problem with the same thinking we
used to create it.

Perhaps fear is holding you back. Maybe you have
become a slave to the what-ifs. *What if I try a different
way of solving this problem and I fail? What if it doesn't
work out? What if I make the wrong decision?*

Not deciding is making a decision to do the same thing again expecting a different result. It is making a decision to get more of what you already have.

There are two ways to tackle any problem in your life: through fear or through faith. When you choose fear, you choose bondage to the problem and more of the same old same old. When you choose faith, you open the door to pure potentiality.

Buddha tells us that the mind is the slayer of the real. Fear comes from your thoughts, and you can change your mind. In fact, you're the only one who can.

Try a new approach. Step into the unknown.

The answer is out there.

15

Relationships

· ·

> You are the average of the five people you spend the
> most time with.
>
> —Jim Rohn

You're making a mental list right now, aren't you?

Go one better: right now, stop and make an actual,
written list of your Fave Five. This quick exercise will
give you some valuable insight into your life.

The underlying message is that who you choose to
spend your time with dramatically impacts who you
become. Are you spending your time with lots of
Debbie Downers, those people for whom negativity is
a way of life? Does your group consist of drama queens
and kings who thrive on gossip? Do your friends
support your hopes and dreams, or are you surrounded
by fear-based saboteurs who believe they are doing
you a favor by giving you a reality check? Or do you
keep company with world-weary sleepwalkers who
trudge through life in a general state of unhappiness,
yet are unwilling to change?

Misery loves company. Negativity breeds negativity. We all know the clichés. But maybe the reason they are so overused is because they are absolutely true. Negative people have negative thinking and give off negative, stressful energy. Scientists have recently discovered conclusively that brain cells can die from prolonged stressful energy.

Your brain grows on what you feed it. Are you fueling it with positive, healthy friendships and relationships?

Your life depends on it.

16

Perseverance

. . . .

If you're going through hell, keep going.
—Winston Churchill

No matter what you're experiencing right now, one fact always remains: the only way *out* is *through*.

Life never came with a guarantee that it would be easy. If you stop to think about it, we would never develop noble qualities like courage, candor, and heroism if we lived in Utopia. We wouldn't even need them. Every day would be the same—one big *Groundhog Day*, over and over and over, ad nauseam.

The difficulties and trials that we experience act as sandpaper, shaping us into the people we become. In those defining moments, we prove our integrity. We build character. We gain wisdom.

We can't know hot without cold, happy without sad, good without bad, or heaven without hell. So if you are in the valley of despair, keep climbing. The view from the top will be worth it.

It has been said that when one door closes, somewhere another door opens for you. True, but it sure can be hell in the hallway!

Keep going. There's a light at the end of the tunnel.

It's not just a train.

17

Valentine's Day

· ·

All you need is love.

—John Lennon

Did you know that Valentine's Day is part of Random Acts of Kindness Week? It's a great time to take the Extreme Kindness Challenge.

For the next week, perform one random act of kindness daily. Remember to keep it to yourself, for your true character is revealed when you think no one is looking.

Imagine the possibilities if everyone reading this right now followed through with one random, kind act each day for seven days.

Short on ideas? Keep it simple. Hold the door for a stranger. Clean the snow off someone's car. Pay a toll for another driver. Shovel for an elderly neighbor. Give praise to a child. And remember to offer a smile to everyone—a smile is a love weapon so powerful that you can even break ice with it.

As comedian Jim Gaffigan tells us, without Valentine's Day, February would be . . . well, January! Let's celebrate.

Have a *love*ly day.

President's Day

<big>**18**</big>

. . . .

> You are here to enrich the world. You impoverish yourself if you forget this errand.
>
> —Woodrow Wilson

Did you know that President's Day is always celebrated on the third Monday in February?

Woodrow Wilson left us with the profound words above to live by, a reminder to use the gifts that are unique to each one of us in service to something greater than ourselves. A gift is not a gift until you give it away.

Teddy Roosevelt echoed this sentiment when he told us, "Do what you can, with what you have, where you are." There's something that only you can do, in a way that no one else can. Since there will never again in the history of the world be another one of you, it's time to share yourself with the world. If you don't, who will?

Franklin Delano Roosevelt said, "To reach a port, we must sail—sail, not tie at anchor—sail, not drift."

You are on a mission to enrich the world. Pull up the anchor. Push away from the dock. Sail. You're here now, alive now, and you are a once-in-a-lifetime edition. Go on. It's your time.

Harry S. Truman made this observation: "It is amazing what you can accomplish if you do not care who gets the credit." It doesn't matter, does it? Because we only impoverish *ourselves* when we withhold our gifts and talents from the world.

And finally, Abraham Lincoln said, "In the end, it's not the years in your life that count. It's the life in your years." Your life counts. What you do matters. Put some life in your years by finding the best in you and sharing it.

It's time to run an errand for the president.

19

Self-Love

· ·

I have never loved another person the way I loved myself.

—Mae West

Good for you, Mae West. I like how you think.

Your best relationship should be the one you have with yourself. There is no other relationship that is more important. The only person who is with you forever is *you*. There is nothing more permanent than your own company. You came in together, and you're going out together. Might as well get along!

The sobering fact is that parents die, children grow up and move away, friends go their separate ways, and marriages sometimes end. But if you love yourself, you'll always have your best friend right there beside you.

Lucille Ball once said that her secret to success was that she loved herself first and then everything else just fell into line. Try it and see. Cultivate love for yourself. Try not to hold yourself to some ridiculous standard that you would never dream of imposing on anyone else. Cut yourself some slack and love the skin you're in.

It's yours for life, and you wear it well.

Making Decisions

20

• •

Advice is what we ask for when we already know the answer but wish we didn't.

—Erica Jong

Do you suffer from analysis paralysis—weighing decisions out again and again, only to come to no conclusion at all? Do you then ask others to advise you, adding their opinions to your confusion? *I used to be indecisive; now I'm just not sure . . .*

Not making a decision is, in fact, making a decision to *not* decide. Too often we turn to others for help, yet they're having difficulty managing their own lives.

It has been said that unless you shape your life, someone else will shape it for you. With your one and only life at stake, it's essential that you learn to listen to your innate intuition about what is truly best for you.

It takes time and patience to learn to listen to your own advice. Maybe you'll make a few mistakes along the way, but since the road to success is always under construction, you're going to learn a lesson or two while on your detour. And you're bound to feel empowered with each choice you make on your own.

While it's important to make intuitive as well as educated decisions, it was once wisely stated that an ounce of intuition is worth a pound of tuition. Experience is, after all, still our best teacher.

Be a little wiser. Be your own advisor.

21

Individuality

· ·

You were born an original. Don't die a copy.

—John Mason

If you're reading this right now, you're a fellow oxygen-breathing mammal.

Isn't it nice to know that we at least have that in common? There may be times when you're dealing with neighbors or colleagues who seem like they're only visiting this planet. Sound familiar? That little tidbit of information in the opening sentence may be your starting point as you desperately try to think of *any way* that the two of you could ever be alike.

At all times, though, you should appreciate and celebrate your individuality. No one in the history of the world will ever have your fingerprints. Doesn't that astound you? There are well over seven million people in the world, and not one of them has your fingerprints or your tongue print, either. That makes each one of us unprecedented, a perfect specimen.

It makes you look at everyone with a little more reverence, knowing that you are walking the earth with someone who will never again exist in the history of the world. Kind of makes you want to get everyone's autographs, doesn't it?

Judy Garland was once quoted as saying, "I'd rather be a first-rate version of myself than a second-rate version of someone else." She was a once-in-a-lifetime celebrity, just like you.

Applaud your *you*-niqueness. Enjoy it! Exalt it! Better start giving (and getting) some autographs.

Be an original.

22

Worry

· ·

> You cannot prevent the birds of worry from flying over
> your head, but you don't have to let them make a nest
> in your hair.
>
> —Chinese proverb

Better go get a mirror. Is it a bad hair day?

Has anything nested in your hair today—worries about your job, your health, your relationships, your family, your future?

Your mind grows on what you feed it. If you are giving it a constant diet of anxieties and worries, you are fueling a fearful mind. When you choose to live in worry of what tomorrow will bring, you live in fear.

It has been said that *fear* stands for *false evidence appearing real*. In other words, you are creating a false reality when you wring your hands and lose sleep over a future that probably won't even come to pass. Choosing fear takes the power out of the present moment. The past is over and the future hasn't happened. Choosing to live by faith allows you to

41

accept the most basic of concepts: the only constant in life is change.

Mark Twain said, "I have known a great many troubles, but most of them never happened." Take a moment to reflect upon your own life. What did you worry about ten years ago? How many of those worries came true?

There is no such thing as security in nature. Birds wake up every day, not knowing where their next meal will come from, but they sing anyway. What a great way to start your day: worry-free, with a song in your heart!

Let your hair down.

Control

· ·

For peace of mind, we need to resign as General
Manager of the Universe.

—Larry Eisenberg

Think you might be a CEO—controlling *every* *one*?
Read on. Here are some signs that you may be suffering
from *controlfreakosis*:

1. When watching television, you *must* have the
   remote at all times.
2. If traveling in a car, you *must* be the driver. If
   not, you'll complain the entire time.
3. No one can load the dishwasher as well as you can.
4. They can't fold the laundry the right way, either.
5. Might as well do it all yourself if you want it done
   right (heavy sigh, hand stuck to forehead).
6. You feel resentful that others are relaxing while
   you have to fix their mistakes.

If any of that sounds familiar, it might be time to hand
in your resignation as GM. Relax. What's the worst
that can happen if the socks are inside out? Will the
world end if the bowls aren't lined up by size in the

dishwasher? If your car is parked slightly crooked in the driveway, will it matter next year at this time?

There are only 86,400 seconds in a day. Don't waste a single one worrying about everything being done your way. You learned to do things by trial and error. You had to learn how to crawl, and then walk, and then run. Another person can tell us all day long how to drive a stick shift, but we never learn until we get behind the wheel and stall on a few hills. Let others learn from their mistakes too.

You can do it. Give your notice. Throw in the towel. Abdicate your GM throne.

Ahhhh . . . feel that? It's called peace of mind.

Breathe easy.

24

Gossip

· ·

> You can't keep people from having a bad opinion of
> you, but you can keep them from being right about it.
> —Author unknown

It's a fact of life. People talk about other people. That means that someone has been talking about you. Feels kind of weird, doesn't it?

What are they saying? Is it bad or good? True or false? *Is this just one more thing for me to worry about ?*

Don't torture yourself. Ralph Waldo Emerson once posed this very insightful question: "Why should my happiness depend on the thoughts going on in someone else's head?" (or the words coming out of their mouths, for that matter).

Sooner or later, we all have our turn in the hot seat. Here's the deal: What someone else thinks of you or says about you means nothing unless *you* make it your truth.

Dr. Wayne Dyer has been widely quoted as saying, "What other people think of me is none of my business." Try to become independent of the bad *and* the good opinions of others. You can give another meaning to "live above the influence."

Raise your own bar. Be your own cheering section. Live up to your own high expectations. Make sure that someday when your life flashes before your eyes, you're proud of what you're watching.

They might be talking, but you don't need to listen.

Ready? Block your ears.

La la la la la . . . I can't hear you!

25

Anger and Resentment

· ·

Hanging onto resentment is letting someone you despise
live rent-free in your head.

—Ann Landers

What kind of landlord are you? Has someone moved
into your head who shouldn't be there?

When you spend time holding on to anger and
resentment, reliving it over and over again in your
mind, the only person you hurt is yourself. The person
you're angry at is probably at home sleeping like a
baby, completely unaware that you're fuming mad
across town.

Anger, hostility, and resentment are physically
dangerous for our bodies. While you may feel like
your blood is boiling, it is actually coagulating more
quickly. Inflammation increases throughout your
body. Blood pressure and blood sugar increase, while
immunity is lowered. This type of hostility increases
levels of hormones that double the risk of coronary
artery disease and triple the risk of heart attack.
Chronic anger is considered to be as dangerous a risk

factor as smoking when it comes to causes of early death.

Is the person you are angry at really worth dying for?

Remember, that individual's life is not being shortened at all because *you* are upset. As Buddha once said, "Holding on to anger is like drinking poison and expecting the other person to die."

Who's living in your head? Maybe it's time to give out some eviction notices. Change the locks if you have to. Choose your new tenants wisely.

Get some cardboard boxes, and start up the moving van.

Guilt

26

. . . .

If you're living in the city of guilt and regret, it's time
to get a new address.

—Joyce Meyer

Are you a travel agent—continually sending yourself
on guilt trips? Put your luggage down. Your flight has
been cancelled.

Maybe you're feeling guilty about something you did
in the past. Fact: you cannot change the past by feeling
guilty. Whatever you've done, just don't do it again.
Resolve to live by the saying, "When you lose, don't
lose the lesson."

Perhaps you are feeling guilty about not living up to
your own expectations. Remorse over eating Girl
Scout cookies for dinner does not eliminate the calorie
content. Stop berating yourself. Berating does not
burn extra calories. Instead, as soon as you begin to
feel guilty, acknowledge it and use it as a motivator
for positive change.

Sometimes we like to bring family and friends along on our trips by manipulating them with guilt. Try not to be a guilt-trip tour guide. Misery loves company. Decide not to be miserable.

Guilt can act as a moral compass by reminding us *not* to do what makes us feel awful. In the 1960s and '70s, the catchphrase was, "If it feels good, do it." Ergo, if it doesn't feel good . . .

Don't do it!

Perseverance

. . . .

27

> The greatest oak was once a little nut who held its
> ground.
>
> —Author unknown

A tiny acorn will become a mighty oak tree, growing
up to one hundred feet tall and living for two hundred
or more years. What a legacy left by one little nut!

It's finally spring. It's time to get out our seed packets
and then tend them until they are ready to plant in the
ground. We'll water them, weed them, care for them,
and wait patiently as they grow.

We won't rush them and plead with them and beg them
to hurry up and pull them out of the ground before
they are ready. No amount of yelling at a tomato will
make it ready to eat any faster. We would never dream
of demanding that our plants try harder. A flower
blossoms when it blossoms.

A garden can teach us a valuable lesson. Sometimes in
life we are sowing seeds, sometimes we are tending
developing plants, and sometimes we are reaping the

harvest. All the stages are good. All the stages are essential. There is a season for everything.

Let's give another meaning to "Season's Greetings." Whatever season you're in, greet it with enthusiasm and patience, because this, too, shall pass.

Nuts unite!

Happiness

28

• •

The pursuit of happiness is a most ridiculous phrase: if
you pursue happiness you'll never find it.

—C. P. Snow

Happiness: you can't buy it, earn it, own it, travel to
it, or marry it.

There is no material item that will bring you a lifetime
of joy. A corner office with your name on the door is
not the answer. Happiness is not waiting for you on a
tropical island. The perfect man or woman will never
right all your internal wrongs.

Perhaps you find yourself saying, "I'll be happy when
I _____." You can probably think of a way to
fill in that blank. *I'll be happy when I lose ten pounds,
get a raise, meet my soul mate, have a bigger house, a new
car* . . . the possibilities are endless. It's a vicious cycle
that does not lead to happiness. It forces our focus on
the future, so instead of appreciating what we do have,
we long for some magical time when all things will be
perfect. George Fisher wisely noted, "When you aim
for perfection, you'll discover it's a moving target."

Happiness is a state of mind where you should take up residence. After all, it was just rated the third most livable state in the country, right behind Peace (number one) and Ecstasy (a close second)! The school system is great and the taxes are low.

It's easy to move from crappy to happy. You're only one thought away.

Complaining

29

. . . .

I can't complain, but sometimes I still do.

—Joe Walsh

Exciting news: There is now a medicine on the market to treat constant complainers!

It's called an anti-*talks*-idant. Just one spray on those who grumble and moan constantly will stop negative verbal diarrhea for up to eight hours, which coincidentally is the length of a workday. Not enough? Try Pepto Dismal. Four ounces before meals will cure endless bellyaching and general gloominess. Share it with your colleagues! Take it yourself!

Just for today, take the Eeyore challenge: When tempted to dwell on your ailments, real or imagined, make the conscious effort to stop yourself. Ask yourself whose life is better from knowing that you have an upset stomach, feel tired, don't want to be at work, got stuck in traffic, or hate the weather. Ask if this is how you want to spend your precious energy. Try this for one day.

Remember, as well, not to engage in this type of conversation. People will either feel better or worse after a conversation with you. Make the obvious choice.

Anthony J. D'Angelo said, "If you have time to whine and complain about something, then you have the time to do something about it." Are your words diseased, killing your time and infecting those around you? The cure is simply to choose more positive and healing words.

Somewhere today there will be a gathering of the Whiners-and-Diners Club. Consider dropping your membership. At the very least, take your Pepto Dismal before you eat.

Bon appétit!

Seize the Day

30

· ·

> Here is a test to find whether your mission on Earth is finished: if you're alive, it isn't.
>
> —Richard Bach

Congratulations! You woke up alive. You have been graciously granted another day, another chance. There is unfinished work for you to do.

It's time for some spring cleaning—time to take your life's mission down from the shelf, dust it off, and have another look at it. What big plans or great ideas have you shelved that are patiently awaiting your attention?

Maybe it's time to discard some old worn-out thoughts and beliefs that no longer fit you. Throw out the self-imposed limitations right along with them. They just don't suit you. Try on a new attitude.

Do a little internal housework. Clean up any messes you've made, starting today. It has been said, "Though no one can go back and make a brand-new start, anyone can start from now and make a brand-new ending."

Death is hereditary. But a little housework never killed anyone.

Carpe diem.

Change

31

. . . .

When your horse is dead, it's time to dismount.

—Rick Warren

We know that change is inevitable. Struggle, however, is optional. The time has come to use some good old-fashioned horse sense, stop struggling, and dismount.

Is there a situation in your life that's dead—a job, relationship, personal habit, or mind-set, perhaps? If you're unable to breathe life into it, perhaps you need to give it a decent burial.

Jim Knight said, "You've got to stop whipping a dead horse sometime." He must be a fellow equestrian who knew when to throw in the towel.

Avoiding your dead horse does not make it disappear. Convincing yourself to invest even more time does not bring your dead horse back to life. Dead is dead. Couldn't all this energy be used better elsewhere?

Take the reins in your hands. Get a new horse. Ride off into the sunset.

Giddyap!

Beginning

32

• •

> You don't have to be great to start, but you have to start
> to be great.
>
> —Joe Sabah

Once upon a time, you didn't know how to talk. You couldn't feed yourself. You didn't know how to read.

Not so very long ago, you didn't know what "just Google it" meant. And more recently, you added texting and maybe even blogging and tweeting to your repertoire of skills. Now it's a piece of cake.

Think of something that was once difficult for you that you now do without giving it a second thought. "All things are difficult before they are easy," said Dr. Thomas Fuller, who incidentally wasn't born a doctor and probably wasn't great at the start. Somebody had to be his first patient!

Everyone who is now a master was once a novice. What would you try if you knew you could not fail? Is it time to step outside of your comfort zone onto the path that leads to greatness? Maybe there's an inner musician, artist, or athlete waiting patiently inside of you. You're on the clock, and time's tickin'.

Your history starts now.

Mistakes

· ·

33

> Wisdom usually comes with age, but sometimes age comes all by itself.
>
> —Judge Alex

Making mistakes is a fact of life. The best-case scenario is that we are left a little wiser than we were before. If mistakes are the vehicle we take to go from novice to sage, then our license plate reads, "Experience."

When you make a mistake, think of a professional baseball player. Their errors are not only counted but then published and announced for the entire world to see and hear. It would certainly be disheartening if you were to pick up the newspaper and read headlines detailing each error you made in the game of life.

The message is clear. As John Powell stated, "The only real mistake is the one from which we learn nothing."

Wouldn't it be great to be a meteorologist? Then you could make mistakes at work and blame them on Mother Nature!

34

Your Life Story

. . . .

My life has a superb cast, but I can't figure out the plot.

—Ashleigh Brilliant

If all of life is a stage, you can either sit in the audience or win the Tony award for a leading role. As Dr. Wayne Dyer often says, "This isn't a dress rehearsal."

If all of life is a book and you are the author of your own story, then you have the ability to write a classic, a masterpiece. You can also write in or write out any character of your choosing. Ahhh. Feel the power?

And since there is no way to know how the story ends, it makes perfect sense not to worry about the final act or the last page. You know it's coming. Make the book so interesting that you can't put it down. Play the role of your life with such passion that when the curtain falls, your adoring fans will demand an encore.

Break a leg!

35

New Day

· ·

I intend to live forever. So far, so good.

—Steven Wright

If you're reading this, you woke up on the right side of the dirt today. What a privilege to have the gift of one more day.

You just won the jackpot: another chance. With each sunrise, you get the miracle of another twenty-four hours. Consider yourself abundantly blessed by this extraordinary opportunity.

John Wayne once said, "Tomorrow is the most important thing in life. Comes into us at midnight very clean. It's perfect when it arrives and it puts itself in our hands. It hopes we've learned something from yesterday."

It's here. It's the tomorrow that you worried about yesterday. Don't waste a precious moment. You'll never get to live this particular day again.

You're holding in your hands a clean slate.

What will you write on this new day?

36

Change

· ·

It's a very slow process - two steps forward, one step
back - but I'm inching in the right direction.

—Rob Reiner

It's not always about willpower. Sometimes even when
you know you need to make changes, you end up
listening to the same old senseless, harmful, intrusive
thoughts that are only going to get you more of what
you already have. Your willpower gets lost in the
vicious circle. You feel like you're losing ground.

Is your brain full of *s*enseless, *h*armful, *i*ntrusive
*t*houghts?

If so, you're not alone. So many of us spend our
precious time having negative conversations in our
minds, berating ourselves for having that piece of
cake, losing our temper, or driving right past the
gym after work. Making a lasting change begins
with changing our internal dialogue, one baby step
at a time. If you've ever seen the movie *What About
Bob?*, you'll know that it's all about: ". . . baby

steps to Lake Winnipesaukee." Great advice, Bill Murray.

Just for today, put one foot in front of the other. Take that first baby step.

Inch by inch, it's a cinch!

Priorities

37

• •

> Being the richest man in the cemetery doesn't matter to
> me. Going to bed at night saying we've done something
> wonderful . . . that's what matters to me.
>
> —Steve Jobs

Contrary to the popular T-shirt sentiment, he who dies
with the most toys does not win. It will never say on
your gravestone, "Here lies _____, whose truck
had a Hemi," or ". . . who owned three Coach bags."
Your legacy has nothing to do with your possessions.
Your giant flat-screen plasma TV will not remember
you when you're gone. It also does not hug back.

More things you won't read after your name on a
gravestone include ". . . who never lost that last ten
pounds" or ". . . who should have put more hours in
at the office."

What you'll leave behind is the legacy of a being a
loving friend, son, daughter, brother, sister, mother,
or father. Those are the kinds of things that make it
to the gravestone.

He who dies with the most joys wins.

38

Procrastination

· ·

All the Woulda-Coulda-Shouldas

Layin' in the sun,

Talkin' 'bout the things

They woulda-coulda-shoulda done . . .

But those Woulda-Coulda-Shouldas

All ran away and hid

From one little *did*.

—Shel Silverstein

Hindsight is 20/20. No doubt about it.

However, there's a reason why our eyes are located on the front of our bodies: we are meant to look forward while stepping bravely into the daily unknown, not stare woefully at our past trash heap of failures. In fact, we shouldn't spend our time looking back unless we plan to go that way.

Pat Riley said, "There's no such thing as coulda, shoulda, or woulda. If you shoulda and coulda, you woulda done it." Okay, so there are some things you would change if you had the chance. But you don't. Any time spent wishing this to be different changes absolutely nothing. A decision to move forward, on the other hand, changes everything. It is not only the antidote to despair but also the anti-shoulda-woulda-coulda.

Start today by living your life so that the only regret you'll have is that you didn't do this sooner. The present perfect is not just a tense in English grammar. The present is perfect, a perfect place, the *only* place to start.

The present is a gift.

Taking Action

39

. . . .

Nothing changes until something moves.

—Albert Einstein

We all know that Einstein knew his way around the universe. So if you're feeling a little stuck and world-weary, maybe Albert's words of wisdom will help the earth move for you.

Oftentimes it's easier to complain about our circumstances than to make a move. We get stuck on life's waiting list: waiting for a sign, waiting for the timing to be right, waiting for things to be perfect—always waiting, afraid to make a false move. But as W. L. Bateman once said, "If you keep on doing what you've always done, you'll keep on getting what you've always got."

Get your name off the waiting list and onto the to-do list. If it's time to move on, move up, or move out, make your move. You already know what to expect if you do nothing: more time in life's waiting room with an old magazine.

Good things may eventually come to those who wait, but they come faster to those who take action. It's time to move some proverbial mountains, one shovelful at a time. Can you dig it?

Bust a move!

Truth

40

· ·

A lie may take care of the present, but it has no future.

—Author unknown

The truth—just think of all the things that we do to it!

We bend it, stretch it, deny it, and hide it. Sometimes we tell it in halves or get it in grains. It can be tarnished or unvarnished. It can be gospel, and it can even be naked. But the most valuable thing we can do with the truth is face it.

The worst lies are the ones we tell ourselves. Ignoring the truth doesn't stop it from being the truth. A Yiddish proverb reminds us that, "A half-truth is a whole lie." Are you being authentic with yourself? And if not, why not?

We lie to ourselves when we are afraid. Maybe we lie because we don't know what to do and ignoring the truth buys us some time. Maybe we are afraid of what others may think, so we live a lie that we start to believe. Or we live in fear that some secret truth of ours will be discovered, thereby giving it more power as we use precious energy to conceal it. Have you forgotten that the truth shall set you free?

Since a large percentage of disease is rooted in anxiety, negativity, and fear-based thought patterns, doesn't it make sense to start by telling the truth, the whole truth, and nothing but the truth to yourself? Fear paralyzes. Truth empowers. To thine own self be true.

Veritas curat. Truth cures.

Just the facts, ma'am.

Don't Quit

41

. . . .

Failure is the path of least persistence.

—Author unknown

It doesn't take any particular talent to quit. In fact, anyone can do it.

Perseverance, on the other hand, means hurling yourself over obstacles, enduring hardship and even pain. But while pain is temporary, the anguish of quitting lasts forever.

Think of water. At 211 degrees, water is hot. However, one extra degree changes everything. When water reaches 212 degrees, it boils, and steam is produced. Steam is used to transmit energy. Steam engines were the foundation of the Industrial Revolution, powering factories, trains, and boats. All this from one extra degree.

Earn your degree by giving the extra effort. Go the extra mile. It's worth the walk.

Pavement pounders prevail!

42

Veteran's Day

• •

> This nation will remain the land of the free only so long
> as it is the home of the brave.
>
> —Elmer Davis

Imagine what your life would be like without freedom.

While you were asleep last night, there were US soldiers being shot at or ambushed in Afghanistan and Iraq. These are people just like you who are far away from the comforts of home, family, and friends.

The original Armistice Day, now Veteran's Day, was observed after World War I. Our soldiers have served in six major wars since then to preserve our way of life here at home. Many lives have been lost so that we can continue to enjoy the liberty that we often take for granted.

We observe Veteran's Day on November 11. Let us never forget to be grateful for our freedom each morning when we awaken from a deep and restful sleep. It is made possible by the brave individuals who stand guard over our freedom.

Celebrate Veteran's Day every day. Remember to thank a veteran.

Freedom isn't free.

43

Decisions

· ·

> When the beard catches fire, it is not very smart to pray
> for rain.
>
> —Paramanhansa Yogananda

Are you sitting on the proverbial fence, wondering which way to jump? Have you weighed your options so many times that even the scale is tired of you?

Sometimes when we have a tough decision to make, it's easy to convince ourselves to wait, hoping that something will happen to tip the scales and decide for us. We bide our time, looking for signs, hoping for anything that will give us a push off our perch.

Yesterday ended at midnight. If you spent one more sleepless night on that uncomfortable fence, you deserve better sleeping arrangements tonight. You can't make progress without making decisions. If nothing ever changes, nothing ever changes.

If your beard is on fire, maybe it's time to shave. Now, is it better to shave *with* the grain or *against* it? Sounds like another decision.

But first, put out the fire.

44

Thanksgiving

· ·

> Feeling gratitude and not expressing it is like wrapping
> a present and not giving it.
>
> —William Arthur Ward

Thanksgiving Day is upon us. And though we know that we should be grateful for each and every day in between, sometimes we get busy. We take things—and people—for granted. In fact, we are sometimes nicer to complete strangers than we are to our own family members.

Maybe it's easy for you to hug a friend or give a word of encouragement to a colleague. Have you done the same for your spouse or children today?

Maybe it's easy for you to be a team player at the office, making compromises as needed to create a better work environment. Are you doing the same in your own home?

Human beings have only a finite number of heartbeats. On this Thanksgiving Day, make a promise to yourself to tell those people in your life that you are grateful for them. It's better to say it now than regret that you could have, but never did.

Thank them all—family, friends, coworkers, the dry cleaner, that person who always makes your coffee the right way . . . the opportunities are endless.

Find a little time in each day for *thanks giving*—two words.

Know Thyself

45

· ·

> After college, I didn't want a job. I wanted to find myself.
> So I went to India, where I thought I might be.
> —Sir Ken Robinson

Inner space: the final frontier. Yet we look everywhere but inside to find ourselves.

How to find yourself in two easy steps:

1. Turn off.
2. Tune in.

Step one involves unplugging yourself from everything so you can hear the still, small voice within. It's impossible to hear that voice when you are simultaneously texting, blogging, Facebook-ing, taking pictures with your phone, and wearing earbuds. Remember the rule: garbage in, garbage out. Guard carefully what you allow to grow in the fertile field of your mind.

Step two involves learning to listen once you've turned off the sensory stimuli. Try starting slowly, with fifteen minutes of silent reflection each morning. You'll be surprised at what you will hear. "Some days, we just need to turn the quiet up," said Dr. SunWolf.

Are you ready to explore a strange new world? To boldly go where no one has gone before? You don't need to go to the ends of the galaxy. The trip of a lifetime awaits you right here at home. Travel lightly. Go inside.

Beam me *in*, Scotty!

46

Time

. . . .

Time may be a great healer, but it's a lousy beautician.

—Anonymous

Oh, the things we do with time!

We borrow it, mark it, pass it, serve it, spare it, spend it, waste it, and kill it. We try to fight it, race against it, and stitch it. We describe it as right, wrong, good, bad, hard, rough, tough, and quality. It can even be a pilot, because we think it can fly. Sometimes we get lost in the mists of it. All this for something we can't see, touch, or stop.

Carl Sandburg said, "Time is the coin of your life. It is the only coin you have, and only you can determine how it will be spent. Be careful lest you let other people spend it for you."

Each second of each day represents a new chance for change. What a coincidence that a coin means *change*.

How will you spend your coin today?

Time to make change!

Holiday Season Stress

47

. . . .

> How can a society that exists on instant mashed potatoes, packaged cake mixes, frozen dinners, and instant cameras teach patience to its young?
>
> —Paul Sweeney

With Thanksgiving leftovers still on the stove, we rushed off to start Black Friday two hours earlier this year. We were just too impatient to wait the extra 120 minutes. Should we now call this Gray Thursday? Can White Wednesday be too far behind? What happened to having a little patience?

During this season, we rush to buy, wrap, and deliver gifts; send cards; and attend parties and family get-togethers—and then we complain that we have no Christmas spirit. It's no wonder. We barely got through dessert, and Gray Thursday was whispering in our ears, "Hurry up."

Patience is still a virtue, and it's time to stop the madness. If you're running full speed on the holiday treadmill, slow your pace. Stroll leisurely through this holiday season and enjoy the gift of presence. And what a present it is!

Ignore the Valentine's Day candy in aisle eight.

48

Christmas Spirit

. . . .

> I wish we could put up some of the Christmas spirit in
> jars and open a jar of it every month.
>
> —Harlan Miller

Wouldn't it be great if you could go into your pantry and take out a jar of humanity to use in the middle of March?

Here's the good news: instead of letting the bottles of forgiveness and understanding gather dust on a shelf, only to be used at Christmastime, you can use a little each day and never run out. The miraculous thing about these products is that the more you use, the more you'll have. It's like a bottomless cup of coffee, but better for you—and for everyone else too.

Here's the catch: you have to remember to use them. It's easy to get into the spirit of things in December when everyone else is doing it. But don't pack up your jar of Christmas spirit and tuck it away in the attic with the holiday ornaments immediately after the gifts are opened and the tree is down. Charles Dickens wrote, "I will honor Christmas in my heart, and try to keep it all the year."

Keep a can of kindness open all year 'round. Be kind to yourself—have a heaping spoonful each day, and then serve generous helpings to others. And have yourself a merry little Christmas every day!

Be the gift.

49

New Year

. . . .

> What the New Year brings to you depends a great deal
> on what you bring to the New Year.
>
> —Vern McLellan

The best resolution to make this year may involve no special purchase of expensive exercise equipment that may become a coat rack by March, or diet foods that resemble colored cardboard and arrive at your house by mail. Instead, maybe the best resolution is one that requires no financial investment at all.

What if we were all just nice to each other?

We have a clean slate. It's called a new year. Can you even imagine a world where everyone really and truly treated others as they would like to be treated? It's got to start somewhere. Why not with you, me, all of us?

It's so crazy, it just might work.

I'm in. Are you with me?

50

Envy

• •

> Comparison is the thief of joy.
>
> —Theodore Roosevelt
> (also attributed to Dwight Edwards)

Turn on the TV, and you'll notice how we are constantly bombarded by commercials promoting images of many of the things we don't have in our lives but wish we did: chiseled abs, wrinkle-free foreheads, sleek new sports cars, fantasy vacations.

Why are we never satisfied with the thighs we came with? Will a faster car really bring us lifelong happiness? Is a Disney cruise the only thing between you and eternal bliss?

When you resent another person for having something you perceive that you are lacking, it's called *comparison*. It's also called *envy*, and that's one of the seven deadly sins. It seems like a darn good idea to avoid anything that has the word *deadly* right in it.

They broke the mold when they made you. There's no room for comparison, because you're the only one of you.

There. Doesn't that take the pressure off?

Arrest the joy stealer.

Fear of Missing Out

51

. . . .

It is far better to be alone than to wish you were.

—Ann Landers

Do you suffer from FOMO?

It's a pop-culture acronym that stands for *f*ear *o*f *m*issing *o*ut on something we perceive as more interesting, exciting, or better than what we're currently doing. Psychologists consider this fear-driven compulsion to text, tweet, and check technology an addiction.

Can you spend a cozy night at home without checking to see if your friends are out having fun somewhere? Do you feel that your simple pleasures pale in comparison to the pictures posted on Facebook by everyone else?

One in every nine people on earth is on Facebook. With Americans spending 53.5 billion minutes on Facebook each month, no wonder we are a nation in the grip of FOMO. Maybe instead of compulsively searching for cyberspace friends and soul mates, we should start by being our own *sole* mates. "You cannot be lonely if you like the person you're alone with," advised Dr. Wayne Dyer.

You need nobody to make you somebody. Start by making friends with yourself.

Solo or FOMO? The choice is yours.

Love the one you're with.

Opportunity

52

> Opportunity's favorite disguise is trouble.
>
> —Frank Tyger

As appealing as it sounds to live in a perpetual paradise, we don't learn much when everything is perfect.

A crisis is a turning point, a decisive moment that challenges us to dig deep and discover the strength within us. Anytime we're faced with a challenging situation, the opportunity for growth is incredible. "I never had a crisis that didn't make me stronger," said football great Louis "Lou" Holtz.

Trouble is nothing more than sandpaper that shapes our lives. All that shaping and smoothing oftentimes reveals an invaluable teacher called Experience, who happens to be a close relative of Wisdom.

Someone's knocking. Who does it look like to you: trouble or opportunity?

It's just a mask.

93

53

Perseverance

· ·

> There is no passion to be found playing small—in settling for a life that is less than the one you are capable of living.
>
> —Nelson Mandela

Have you found your groove? Or has your groove become a rut?

Maybe you've labeled yourself and become a prisoner of past bad habits. Statements like, "I've always been afraid of _____ " or "I've never been able to _____ " only reinforce the low expectations that we impose upon ourselves. And no one rises to low expectations.

If you're feeling tired and defeated, maybe you're clinging to outdated ideas that no longer work in your life. Self-imposed punishing thoughts and negative labels can become oddly comfortable over the years, until we eventually allow them to define us.

Become the architect of your future. Blaze a trail instead of plodding along on the treadmill of life.

Ellen Glasgow said, "The only difference between a rut and a grave are the dimensions." And that sounds pretty grave.

Groove, trail, rut. Two outta three ain't bad.

54

Action

· ·

Even if you're on the right track, you'll get run over if
you just sit there.

—Will Rogers

While patience is considered one of the seven heavenly
virtues, having too much patience can eventually become
inertia. Stagnation did not make the celestial list.

Perhaps you are waiting for conditions to be just right
before you make your big move. There's a point where
waiting is actually indecision. You promise yourself
that you'll take action when the holidays are over,
you've paid off some debt, the kids are grown, you lose
that last ten pounds, and so on. Will you be satisfied
remembering the things that you *planned* to do with
your life?

"You may live or work around a bunch of weeds,
but don't let that stop you from blooming," said Joel
Osteen. If you're waiting for perfect timing, you're
going to have a long wait. Dare to sprout.

Grow where you're planted.

55

Judgment

. . . .

> When nobody around you seems to measure up, it's
> time to check your yardstick.
>
> —Bill Lemley

It's simple to go into the business of fault-finding. You need no particular talent. You need no self-control. You don't need an office. The only piece of equipment you need to open your business is a bar that you set for yourself—at the lowest position.

Finding fault is far easier than recognizing our own shortcomings. We call the mistakes we've made "learning experiences," but we aren't nearly as generous when passing judgment on others. Our self-proclaimed life lessons are dubbed sins for everyone else, as we elect ourselves judge and jury of the world.

"Every saint has a past and every sinner has a future," said Oscar Wilde. At times in our lives, we've all been both. Why try to change other people when we struggle just trying to change ourselves?

The Dalai Lama once said that people take different roads seeking fulfillment and happiness. Just because they're not on your road doesn't mean they've gotten lost. That's good news. They don't need your yardsticks, your road maps, or your GPS.

Hoe your own road.

56

Action

• •

We must be willing to let go of the life we have planned,
so as to accept the life that is waiting for us.

—Joseph Campbell

Holding on for dear life? Holding up under pressure?
Holding off on making a decision? Maybe it's time to
let go.

Whenever we cling too tightly to anything—
whether it's an idea, a relationship, or even a material
item—we sacrifice the opportunity for something
new to come into our lives. It takes a lot of energy
to hang on to things, especially those that have long
since worn out their welcome. Holding on doesn't
necessarily mean that you are a stronger person. It
takes a courageous person to release and surrender
to the unknown.

"You can only lose what you cling to," according to
Buddha. And .38 Special instructed us to "Hold On
Loosely." Wise words from the prophets.

Are you holding out for a hero? Look no further. The hero is you.

Leap and the net will appear.

57

Simplify

· ·

My dog taught me my greatest life lesson: shed a lot.

—Author unknown

Let's try an experiment. Get out a piece of paper and a pencil. Ready?

Make a list of all the things you can take with you when you die. Got it? Now make a list of all the people who won't eventually die.

Your dog isn't worried about whether or not his collar has a little polo player insignia on it. He's not concerned that his tags aren't solid gold. He's happy with the good old basics of food and shelter but happiest when those necessities are accompanied by kindness and love.

Your dog doesn't care if you have a boat or a new master bathroom. He's perfectly content to be patted on an old couch and played with in a yard that isn't professionally landscaped.

Do you really need one more thing to dust, insure, pay off, or store?

The journey through life requires very little baggage. Pack lightly. Keep your dog by your side. And remember to wag your tail and not your tongue!

Happy "tails" to you!

58

Procrastination

· ·

> I'm going to stop putting things off . . . starting tomorrow!
>
> —Sam Levenson

Hold on to your hats, folks! The meeting of the Procrastinators Club has been postponed. Now it's time to ask yourself if you, in fact, are a card-carrying member of this group.

Procrastinators are the leaders of tomorrow. They're convinced that the future is the Promised Land, where there is enough time to chop vegetables for a salad, go to the gym, and get to that stack of mail on the dining-room table. Instead, they end up eating Chips Ahoy and watching reruns of *Two and a Half Men* while dust gathers on their growing pile of bills. They sabotage their own efforts and then suffer from that vicious cycle of guilt and shame

It's really a misconception that procrastinators are lazy. They just give in to what they *want* to do in the moment instead of what they *should* do. They abandon

Plan A without checking into any of the other letters in the alphabet.

Here's Plan B. Remember the Four Ups?

1. Get up.
2. Dress up.
3. Show up.
4. Look up.

A lot can be accomplished just by following this simple plan. Just being present and accounted for is a half the battle. Add showing up with a good attitude, and you win the war on procrastination.

Master Yoda said, "Do or do not. There is no try." Listen, we should!

May the Force be with you.

Silence

59

· ·

Drawing on my fine command of the English language,
I said nothing.

—Robert Benchley

Fun fact: You have two ears and one mouth. Epictetus told us way back in the first century that the reason for this anatomical design was because we should listen twice as much as we speak.

Have you ever regretted something you've said? Sometimes silence can't be improved upon. We all know that silence is golden, but we may forget at critical moments in our lives that talk can be tarnished. We bad-mouth, smart-mouth, or mouth-off, only to end up with the dreaded foot-in-mouth disease.

The cure for this malady is simple. Be careful what you eat and make sure it's not your words. Next time you find yourself talking in circles, stop and reflect. Is this a time for words or for silence? You may not need to have the last word when silence says a mouthful.

"'Tis better to be silent and be thought a fool, than to speak and remove all doubt." Well said, Abe Lincoln. Not only honest but the strong silent type as well!

Play it by ear.

60

Trials

• •

Anybody can pilot a ship when the sea is calm.

—Navjot Singh Sidhu

At any given time, each of us is navigating our way into or out of one of the many storms of life. It's possible that you are right smack in the middle of turbulent weather at this very moment.

Everyone loves the calm before the storm. Homer Simpson calls it "that happy period between the lie and the time it's found out." It's easy to steer our boats during the peaceful times. What kind of captain are you when the seas are rough?

To remain unchanged by changing conditions should be your goal, since change is inevitable. Make up your mind to be the calm before, during, and after the storm.

Instead of waiting for the storm to pass, try your hand at riding the waves. No storm lasts forever. There are tranquil waters ahead. And with each storm you successfully weather, you become a more seaworthy skipper. Remember, the only "I" of the storm is you.

If clouds are gathering, hold on to the helm. It's sunny somewhere.

61

Karma

• •

If you step on people in this life, you're going to come
back as a cockroach.

—Willie Davis

We believe in lots of things that we don't physically
see, like wind or gravity. There's another unseen force
that we should respect.

Karma has been described in a number of ways. You
get what you give. You reap what you sow. What goes
around comes around. It's the Golden Rule in action.
This ethical rule of reciprocity is the basic concept of
most major religions, but even if you don't consider
yourself a religious person, your life will profoundly
change for the better when you follow it.

Next time, before you act, ask yourself this question:
Am I being kind? Is this how I would like to be treated?
Dr. Wayne Dyer tells us that the way people treat you
is their karma, and how you react is yours. Being nice
to someone who bugs you can be difficult, but it's the
most evolved form of pest control.

Do **u**nto **o**thers. The acronym is DUO, and you can't do that solo. Although you're the only driver of your karma, there are passengers along for the ride. Kindness is always the high road. Take it.

Life is a highway.

62

Worrying

. . . .

> Worrying is like a rocking chair. It gives you something
> to do, but it doesn't get you anywhere.
>
> —Glenn Turner

If worrying was an Olympic sport, would you be a contender for a gold medal? Have you been in training, just in case it's added to the next Summer Games?

Perhaps you've heard the expression "worried sick." Chronic worry physically affects your sympathetic nervous system, causing it to release stress hormones that harm your immune, digestive, and cardiovascular systems. Is what you're distressed about worth having a heart attack over?

No one has ever added one day to his or her life by worrying. There are no statues erected to famous worriers. There are no awards given for expertly tormenting yourself. You don't need to go for the gold in misery.

Your anguish starts with a thought, and that's the fault of faulty manufacturing. Next time anxiety rears its ugly head, try making a new thought. After all, you're the supervisor in the factory of your mind. How about mass-producing some positive products? And while you're at it, discontinue worry. There's no market for it anyway.

Here's to quality control!

63

Just Say No

. . . .

> A "no" uttered from the deepest conviction is better
> than a "yes" merely uttered to please, or worse, to avoid
> trouble.
>
> —Gandhi

H-e-e-e-e-r-e's Gandhi, a guy who knew a thing or
two thousand. Are there any people-pleasers out there
who need a pep talk from this timeless sage?

If you've ever desperately wished that you could be
freed from all your obligations to people and things,
maybe it's time to examine your motives. When you
become overcommitted by saying yes to save face,
boost your image, or avoid conflict, the mental result
will be resentment. The physical result will at first be
exhaustion and later, disease. A body can only handle
so much stress.

Check your daily planner. Is it full of things like a
full-time job, committee meetings, peewee football
coaching, graduate-school classes, Girl Scout activities,
meals-on-wheels volunteering, Twilight League
games, spinning classes, book club get-togethers, and

babysitting for friends or family? Saying yes when you should say no will make you sick and tired.

"A man's got to know his limitations," said Dirty Harry Callahan. So, go on and make your day. Maybe less is more.

Stay in the *no*.

64

Late Bloomers

· ·

> There is nothing in a caterpillar that tells you it's going
> to be a butterfly.
>
> —Margaret Fuller

Attention, late bloomers! The path less traveled has been walked by many a noteworthy sojourner.

Harlan "Colonel" Sanders did not start Kentucky Fried Chicken until he was in his early sixties. Grandma Moses first picked up a paintbrush when she was seventy-six. At age seventy-two, Oscar Swahn was not only the oldest Olympian ever but also the oldest medalist at the 1920 games. Emily Post published her famous book *Etiquette* when she was fifty years old. Roget invented the thesaurus at seventy-three. Enough?

Don't write yourself off. A butterfly was once housed in a dull cocoon that resembled a dead leaf. Dried up and wrinkly on the outside doesn't tell anything about the inside.

Don't write anyone else off, either. Baseball player Josh Hamilton did not make his major-league debut until the age of twenty-six because of years of serious drug and alcohol abuse. Johann Wolfgang von Goethe said, "Treat people as if they were what they ought to be and you help them to become what they are capable of being." He was nearly sixty when he published *Faust*.

Diamond or coal? Time is on your side.

No pressure!

65

Letting Go

• •

Sometimes good things fall apart so better things can fall together.

—Marilyn Monroe

Holding on for dear life? Maybe you're clinging to something or someone that needs to make a graceful exit. It's time to relax your grip. You can't catch something better if your hands are already full.

Whether it's a job, a relationship, or even a stage of life, knowing when to let go and move on shows vision, poise, and belief in the future. Think back on your own life for a moment. How many things that seemed bad at the beginning turned out to be some of the best things that ever happened to you?

Seneca said, "Every new beginning comes from some other beginning's end." Both Semisonic and Green Day found this so noteworthy that they sang about it.

Why wait for an emergency to use the exit doors? There's a new start waiting on the other side.

It's closing time.

66

Relax

• •

People say nothing is impossible, but I do nothing every day.

—Winnie-the-Pooh

Attention, all human beings! Are you living up to your namesake and taking the time to just *be*?

If, instead, you are more of a human *do*ing, it may be time to slow down. Learning to do nothing actually takes practice. It means giving yourself permission to be idle. You can't achieve inner peace if you feel too guilty to sit down and relax.

The laundry will still be dirty tomorrow. The lawn can wait. You can wash your car another day. Will your legacy be that you died with the cleanest house?

Put your feet up. Turn your phone off. Do a little bit of nothing, and do it in good conscience. Ignore your inner travel agent, who's dying to send you on a guilt trip.

Ready for a sing-along? Do be do be do . . .

Be!

Fear

67

. . . .

You must do the thing which you think you cannot do.

—Eleanor Roosevelt

Take a moment and recall a time when you were filled with fright. Maybe it was the first time you stood on the end of a diving board. Perhaps it was the first time you sat behind the wheel of a car. Or was it the first time you stood before an audience with a microphone in your hand?

You had a choice then—to turn from the diving board and go back to safer ground, thereby fueling your fear, or to propel your body forward and enter the water, surfacing with an ear-to-ear grin, delighted in the knowledge that you just looked fear in the face and laughed.

As Mark Twain so aptly stated, most of the things we worry about never happen. And each time we face our fears, we gain strength and self-confidence.

So what's holding you back? Could it be that whatever is blocking your path *is* your path? Instead of waiting for the fear to pass, do it afraid.

Go ahead and take a chip off the old roadblock.

Have the last laugh.

68

Personal Growth

• •

> The heart is like a garden. It can grow compassion or
> fear, resentment or love. What seeds will you plant
> there?
>
> —Buddha

For a seed to grow, it needs rich soil, sun, and rain. A thought is grown in much the same way in the fertile planting ground of your mind.

What you sow will grow. Reign over your mind's garden, and sunny thoughts will be the harvest. Optimists live longer and have less heart disease—and probably more friends!

Charles Read once stated, "Sow an act, and you reap a habit. Sow a habit, and you reap a character. Sow a character, and you reap a destiny."

It's time to cultivate your green thumb. Weed out thoughts of defeat and despair. Carefully choose what you plant, and watch what crops up in your life.

Everything's comin' up roses!

69

Friends

· ·

Only your real friends will tell you when your face is dirty.

—Sicilian Proverb

Did you know that genuine friendships are good for your health?

We know that our friends provide emotional support and boost our self-esteem, but people with meaningful social connections also have fewer cardiovascular and immune problems. Recent research has shown, too, that women diagnosed with advanced stages of ovarian or breast cancer live twice as long if they have strong support groups. They also experience less pain throughout their treatments.

It has been said that friends are the relatives you make for yourself. With all the mental and physical benefits of friendship, it makes sense to nurture those ties like your life depended on it, because it just might. It turns out that phone-a-friend really is a lifeline!

Time for a "family" reunion!

70

Truth

• •

> Only the hand that erases can write the true thing.
>
> —Meister Eckhart

Long live the eraser.

The rubber eraser was first used in the late 1700s, but wax and even pieces of bread were previously used to remove unwanted lead or charcoal marks on paper. As long as there have been people, there have been mistakes.

As the author of your life story, you may need a little Wite-Out once in a while. But it's worth it to live authentically. Living half the truth is living a whole lie.

It's not always easy to be honest with yourself. James Garfield said, "The truth will set you free, but first it will make you miserable." The alternative, however, is to spend your life being true to a lie.

Honesty is the best policy, and nobody wants to follow the worst policy. Don't be afraid to do a bit of editing within the story of your life. Pressing the "delete" key may help you to move on and start a whole new chapter.

Get real.

71

Beginnings

· ·

> And suddenly you know: It's time to start something
> new and trust the magic of beginnings.
>
> —Meister Eckhart

Here's a news flash for the newbie: while nothing can replace the wisdom of experience, there are few things more freeing than being a novice.

There is a certain level of expectation that comes with success. The bar is raised, never to be lowered again. And if you make a mistake, there is a widespread belief among your peers that you somehow should have known better. As Winston Churchill told us, "The price of greatness is responsibility."

It is much less expensive to be a beginner. Though you will certainly have a price to pay by enduring some humbling moments, others will be more forgiving and willing to help you.

Don't feel rooked by being a rookie. Enjoy being a beginner—you're in good company. No one else has lived this particular day before either. We're all just a little wet behind the ears. Kind of makes you want to help and forgive all over the place, doesn't it?

Fellow novices take notice: uncertainty is certain. Embrace it. Remember, they don't call it "beginner's luck" for nothing!

72

Signs

• •

End of Construction. Thank you for your patience.

—Tombstone of Ruth Graham
(wife of evangelist Billy Graham)

Wouldn't it be great if all of life's sticky situations came with really obvious signs, like the ones posted on our roadways?

Imagine that you're about to make a colossal career mistake and accept an offer for the wrong job. In the nick of time, you look up and see the "Wrong Way" sign. Whew! Crisis averted. You're on a blind date with someone who seems like your soul mate. Thankfully, you spy the "Dead End" sign, saving you months of heartache. Your teenage child is acting like a two-year-old. Both the "Caution" and "Rough Road" signs give you plenty of warning and time to mentally prepare.

Unfortunately, if you're presently in a "Fog Area," it can be difficult to find a sign. Maybe it's time to "Stop" at a "Rest Area" until the confusion clears. When you take time to "Reduce Speed" and "Yield" to your intuition, that inner voice may be the only sign you need. If life is indeed a highway, this is "One Way" to successfully navigate it.

Don't forget to buckle up.

73

Troubles

• •

Rock bottom became the solid foundation on which I rebuilt my life.

—J. K. Rowling

If your life is on the rocks or you've run into a stone wall, take heart. They don't call it "solid as a rock" for nothing.

Just as a whetstone is used to sharpen knives and blades, perhaps the stony ground of rock bottom is merely honing the tools you'll need to rebuild your life from the ground up. Perhaps it's polishing skills that are essential for you to acquire before you can construct and live comfortably in your forever home—your own skin.

If you've been shaken down to your very foundation, you have been given the opportunity to redesign your life. You are the master craftsman and sole proprietor of where all new construction begins—between your ears.

Nothing is etched in stone. Maybe being between a rock and a hard place isn't so hard after all.

Self-Esteem

· ·

> Sometimes I get the feeling the whole world is against me, but deep down I know that's not true. Some of the smaller countries are neutral.
>
> —Robert Orben

Kickin' a can? Takin' your ball and goin' home? Does your new theme song start with the line, "Nobody likes me, everybody hates me"?

Before you go eat worms, dig this: the Rule of 20-40-60. It may help you to take the focus off of yourself. It goes like this: At age twenty, you care what everyone thinks of you. At age forty, you don't care what anyone thinks of you. And at age sixty, you realize that no one was thinking of you to begin with!

So hold off on throwing that pity party. You'll be the only one in attendance anyway. Laugh and the world will laugh with you. Weep and you cry into the punch bowl alone.

What you give to others is exactly what you get back. Be the life of your party.

You've got the whole world in your hands!

Good Intentions

• •

If and When were planted, and Nothing grew.

—Proverb

The tough row to hoe is paved with good intentions. It's impossible to harvest when you haven't planted. How's your crop yield looking? Have you planted any of the following fruitless seeds of *if* and *when*?

- If I made more money, I would _____.
- If I had more time, I would _____.
- When I retire, I will _____.
- When I lose twenty pounds, I'll _____.

Along with the ifs and whens, you may also be planting garden-variety buts. "I'd like to try _____, but I'm too _____." *Old, young, busy, tired*—fill in the blank. It stands to reason that all of this talk would make one a *But*head.

Barren land is the result of planting nothing. Choose carefully the seeds you sow through your thoughts and deeds to become the farmer who reaps a bountiful harvest. The cream of the crop is yours for the taking.

Hi, hoe! Hi, hoe! It's off to work we go!

76

Anger

· ·

> Holding on to anger is like grasping a hot coal with the
> intent of throwing it at someone else; you are the one
> who gets burned.
>
> —Author unknown

Take away the "D," and the Danger Zone ominously becomes the Anger Zone—and for good reason. Anger and resentment are not only harmful for us mentally, but they lead to some serious physical problems.

Hoping to increase your blood pressure and heart rate? Try getting really upset at the person who cut you off in traffic. Planning to dump toxins into your system and actually make your blood boil? Become outraged when your computer freezes. Slam some doors and yell if you accidentally get the wrong order at Dunkin' Donuts. And while you're at it, raise your blood sugar and clog your arteries by being generally ticked off.

Recent research at the Cancer Treatment Centers of America showed that almost two-thirds of cancer patients identified resentment and inability to forgive as personal issues for them.

Flying off the handle only leads to a bad landing. Blowing your top, fuse, or gasket hurts you, both body and soul. Think before you give someone a piece of your mind. Make sure you can do without it first.

When you see red, stop and use your head!

77

Possibilities

. . . .

> The Wright brothers flew right through the smoke
> screen of impossibility.
>
> —Charles Kettering

Impossibility. Just add an apostrophe and a stroke of the space bar, and presto change-o—it immediately becomes *I'm possibility*!

If *impossible* means *unimaginable*, most of us who were using things like dictionaries and encyclopedias in the early 1990s would have called Google impossible. In fact, it would have been inconceivable to Google something at that time, since most of the world didn't even have the Internet yet. Consider other technologies that we now take for granted, like cell phones and e-mail, which once would have sounded like science fiction.

Unthinkable? Unrealistic? Unbelievable? Maybe it's time to undo the *un*s in your life. What limiting beliefs are holding you back from a world full of impossibilities just waiting to happen?

Take a step in the Wright direction. Let your dreams take flight. Mission: possible!

The sky's the limit.

Perseverance

. . . .

78

Life is not about how fast you run or how high you
climb, but how well you bounce.

—Vivian Komori

If life is indeed a game, are you taking care of the ball?
Do the daily stressors of life have you bouncing off the
wall, or are you on a roll?

It's human nature to want to be bigger, better, and
faster—yet even the fastest runner can fall and fail to
get up. Those who bounce right back when they're
down have learned that true success is determined
by perseverance. When Thomas Edison was asked
about his many failures in inventing the lightbulb,
he replied, "I have not failed. I have just found ten
thousand ways that won't work."

So if you've dropped the ball in some area of your
life—whether it's your job, relationship, or New Year's
resolution to get in shape—don't hang your head in

shame and retire to the bench. Life is not a spectator sport. Participate.

Learn to roll with the punches. Bounce starts with a *be*—so let it. It's time to get back in the game.

The ball's in your court.

79

Victim Mentality

• •

> You only get to be a victim once. After that, you're a
> volunteer.
>
> —Naomi Judd

It's time for a checkup from the neck up. Let's drop in and see what condition your condition is in. Do you have your mind set on playing the victim on the stage of life? Maybe it's time to audition for a new role.

When we refuse to accept personal responsibility for our lives, we relinquish our power to change the very circumstances that imprison us. Once we succumb to the victim mentality in any area, whether at work or in a relationship, we begin to identify with that title.

Are you suffering from "*poor me*" *s*yndrome (we'll call it PMS)? Then it's time to reclaim control of your life. Nobody wants PMS. If you're placing someone else's opinions above your own, begin to listen to your own instincts and gut feelings. Put some boundaries in place. Make some decisions. Stamp the seal of approval on yourself.

It only takes a few steps to go from victim to victor. Start by changing the setting of your mind-set.

Victim or volunteer? The choice is yours.

80

Citizenship

• •

> Democracy is the only system that persists in asking
> the powers that be whether they are the powers that
> ought to be.
>
> —Sydney Harris

Election Day is once again upon us. After months of being interrupted during dinner by computer-assisted telephone calls, it's finally time to go to the polls.

If you are one of the 35 percent of Americans who choose not to exercise your right to vote, take a moment to ponder these peculiar points. It was estimated that 66 million people watched the debates between President Obama and Mitt Romney in October 2012. However, on the lowest-rated ever season of *American Idol*, 132 million votes were cast in the grand finale.

Johann Wolfgang von Goethe said, "Things which matter most must never be at the mercy of things which matter least." While it certainly is nice for the talented *American Idol* Phillip Phillips to skyrocket to number one on America's Top 40, the fate of our country surely trumps his musical career.

Stand up and be counted as one of the lucky citizens of the land of the free and the home of the brave. Face the music. Vote.

Make this place your "home."

81

Veteran's Day

. . . .

> Never in the field of human conflict was so much owed
> by so many to so few.
>
> —Winston Churchill

Calling all free agents and free spirits: it's time to celebrate Veteran's Day!

There are approximately 21.5 million military veterans living in the United States. These heroes served in World War II, the Korean War, the Vietnam War, the Gulf Wars, and Afghanistan. Just as importantly, many of them served during peacetime, keeping our country safe.

There are currently about 314 million people living in the United States. This means that less than 7 percent of our men and women are responsible for protecting the freedoms that many of us take for granted.

Remember those precious few who have defended and continue to defend your rights to the big three: life, liberty, and the pursuit of happiness. When you also consider the freedoms of speech, press, and religion; the rights to vote and bear arms; and the right to equality, saying thank you hardly seems like enough.

I think we're going to need a bigger parade!

82

Thanksgiving

· ·

> We make a living by what we get; we make a life by
> what we give.
>
> —Sir Winston Churchill

Lest we forget, Thanksgiving is not only a holiday, it is
also a verb. How best to be thankful for our blessings?
The answer is right in the word itself: by giving.

In these tough economic times, we may wonder exactly
what it is that we can afford to give. There is one gift
that only you can give—and that is the present of your
presence. Though it will cost you nothing, the return
on your investment will be astounding.

Where to start? Give the gift of a smile, a hug, or a
kind word. Give the gift of your time. Lend a hand
or a listening ear, without expecting anything in
return. Hold out an olive branch. Hold a hand. Hold
your tongue. Share a laugh. Share a meal. Share in
someone's joy or sorrow.

Kindness knows no enemy. Invite it to the dinner table this Thanksgiving as your saving grace. Renew the invitation daily.

Get a life. Give.

83

Facing the Truth

• •

> The first time someone shows you who they are, believe them.
>
> —Maya Angelou

Just for a moment, think of one thing that you would like to change about yourself.

Maybe you'd like to be more patient or less of a human doormat. Would you like to be more organized or less of a neat freak? Perhaps you're trying to lose weight, stick to an exercise program, quit smoking, or even give up chocolate. Now imagine that someone *insists* that you change.

When you stop to consider how difficult it is to change your own habits or idiosyncrasies, you'll quickly abandon the prospect of trying to change someone else. Most of us don't respond well to force, threats, or ultimatums.

You are not obligated to change anyone. It just can't be done. You can, however, change your response to people who push your buttons. This may be as simple as knowing when to change the subject. Or it could be as complicated as recognizing when it is healthier for you to love someone from a distance.

If someone's true colors are showing and they're just not palatable to you, don't tell yourself white lies about what you're seeing. Who deserves your honesty more than you?

Seeing is believing.

84

Success

· ·

> Most people fail in life not because they aim too high
> and miss, but because they aim too low and hit.
>
> —Les Brown

Do you believe that you can predict the future?

A *self-fulfilling prophecy* is a statement that we tell
ourselves that can be either positive or negative. It is
so powerful that it actually alters our actions, thereby
predicting the future for us.

Your words have tremendous power to create or destroy.
Something as socially acceptable as telling yourself
that you hate Mondays can taint your perception of
the events of that particular day of the week. It can
be far more pervasive and harmful, however. If you
repeatedly fill your mind with self-imposed limitations,
you will live down to your own expectations.

Success comes in cans, not in can'ts. Listen carefully to
the conversations that you have with yourself. Untie
the *nots* in your life—*I'm not young enough, not old
enough, not smart enough, not good enough.* Embrace the

possibilities by opening some *cans*—*I can do this. I can succeed. I can make a difference.*

Raise the roof! It's high time to raise the bar. No one profits from pessimism—bar none. Stay on target. Set your sights on a bright future.

Ready? Aim. Fire!

85

Forgiveness

. . . .

Forgive others not because they deserve forgiveness, but
because you deserve peace.

—Jonathan Lockwood Huie

If you're holding a grudge, it's time to put it down.

We construct our own prison of poison when we
refuse to forgive. We build the walls with anger,
resentment, and hatred, and then we commit ourselves
to a sentence of solitary confinement with nothing but
toxic thoughts to keep us company.

The act of forgiveness frees us from the detrimental
effects of hostility and vengeance. Just by breaking out
of this self-made cell of spite, we escape the physical
perils of higher blood pressure; elevated symptoms of
anxiety, depression, and stress; and increased incidence
of alcohol and substance abuse. Is it worth it to suffer
life-threatening symptoms while the person you're
angry at goes scot-free?

Pardoning our perceived persecutors promotes personal
peace. Say that three times fast. Better yet, do it!

86

Crisis

. . . .

> The Chinese use two brush strokes to write the word
> "crisis." One brush stroke stands for danger; the other
> for opportunity. In a crisis, be aware of the danger—but
> recognize the opportunity.
>
> —John F. Kennedy

We are facing any number of crises, both nationally and globally.

First and foremost in our minds is the national crisis of violence in our schools. Blame has been placed on everything from video games to lack of gun control. We've attributed it to lack of faith and loss of family. It seems likely that a variety of conditions have led to the creation of this perfect societal storm.

On the global front, we are experiencing economic crises, food crises, environmental crises, and energy crises. What in the world is happening?

Perhaps we are poised for an epic epiphany: one single defining moment when we gain the courage to do things differently. We are doing a lot of talking, and that's a good start, because there is danger in the type of silence that implies consent.

Thomas Edison said, "Opportunity is missed by most people because it is dressed in overalls and looks like work." It's time for a new world order to restore order to our world, one where kindness and compassion exist and thrive under the Golden Rule.

Do you hear that? It's a golden opportunity knocking.

Many hands make light work.

New Year's Resolutions

87

• •

> Whether we want them or not, the New Year will bring new challenges; whether we seize them or not, the New Year will bring new opportunities.
>
> —Michael Josephson

Resolutions come and go, but the guilt of failure lasts the whole year through. This year, let's make a brand-new kind of resolution—one that strengthens instead of sabotages.

Somewhere out there in the New Year, a storm is brewing with your name on it. Resolve right now to ride the waves of life's challenges that will inevitably arrive. Decide whether the weather will ruffle your feathers or if you'll be the calm in the storm. You may not be able to control the environment, but you can always control the *in*vironment. Don't abandon ship. The sun will shine again.

Somewhere out there in the New Year, a door is waiting with your name on it. Opportunity will knock, but it won't hang around in the hallway waiting for you to answer. Resolve to open some doors—and yourself—to possibilities.

Reader recap? Relax. Receive.

Redo!

People-Pleasing

88

• •

I miss your smile . . . but I miss mine more.

—Laurel House

This just in: You cannot make everyone happy.

Let's face it: some people could win an Academy Award for playing the role of victim. To them, it's better to get negative attention than none at all. Eliciting sympathy becomes the only way that they can interact with others. It would take a pickax to make these people crack a smile.

If you're unable to bring joy to the cast of *The Crying Game*, maybe it's time to change the supporting actors in your life. The field of neuroscience has recently discovered that negative people can actually have a detrimental effect on the physical structure of the brains of those around them. It may be best to wash away these brain-drainers if they're acting out.

Smiling improves your immunity, increases your tolerance for pain, and decreases your level of impatience—even if it's only a *fake* smile. Set the stage for your own happiness and fake it 'til you make it.

Lights, camera, action!

89

Empathy

• •

Life's most persistent and urgent question is, 'What are you doing for others?'"

—Martin Luther King, Jr.

While it's true that awesome ends with *me*, recent research shows alarming evidence that there has been a dramatic decrease in empathetic concern—also known as brotherly love—among our nation's youth.

The renowned news program *60 Minutes* ran a story documenting the new breed of American, one that is 40 percent less empathetic than its counterpart from the 1970s. It seems that while today's young Americans have become more confident and assertive, they have also become more self-absorbed and depressed.

Volunteering to help someone in need just may be the cure. The body experiences a rush of endorphins during and after any selfless act of volunteerism. Endorphins are your body's natural painkillers—as strong as and often stronger than morphine—that not only decrease pain but improve your overall emotional health.

The profound positive effects of volunteerism in older adults are widely documented. Now research is showing that volunteering prevents risky behaviors in teens, increases academic success, and decreases symptoms of mild to moderate depression. It looks like volunteering really does pay!

Walk a mile in someone else's shoes. Help carry the load. We're all in this together.

He ain't heavy, he's my brother.

90

Power

• •

When the power of love overcomes the love of power,
the world will know peace.

—Jimi Hendrix

Ahh, the prophets: Jimi Hendrix—so bold as to write
about love—and Huey Lewis—who shared his own
news about the power of love, which makes the world
go 'round.

The love of power won't keep you warm at night. It
won't dry your tears when you're sad, hold your hand,
or comfort you. If you're a power-seeking workaholic
clawing your way to the top, ask yourself how excited
your desk is to see you on Monday morning. Power
won't greet you at the door with a big hug at the end
of a tough day.

It will never say on your gravestone, "Here
lies _____. She worked sixty hours a week." It
may say, however, "Here lies _____, who was a
wonderful daughter, sister, wife, mother, and friend."
Your desk won't be at your funeral. While you need to

make and spend money to live, you also need to make and spend time to have a life worth living.

Ready to cancel your power trip? People all over the world are now boarding the Love Train. Join them! You can't buy your way onto this train. Your money's no good here, just so you know.

Feel the power?

Finding Fault

91

. . . .

> To belittle, you have to be little.
>   —Kahlil Gibran

Do you know any fault-finders? Now ask yourself this: Are they perfect?

Fault-finders have only perfected the quality of feeling superior. They achieve this by being better players at the Blame Game, using the game pieces of Judge, Jury, and Executioner. The point of the game is to build themselves up while tearing others down—except that everyone loses in the end.

Bad-mouthing is for bad apples with bad attitudes. Before you pick up a pawn in this winner-less contest, ask yourself who will benefit if you decide to play the game. Could any of us ever beat the charges if we were on trial for crimes of imperfection?

Play in the big leagues. Don't belittle.

Let's put the *kind* back in mankind. Are you game?

92

Self-Respect

. . . .

The secret of education lies in respecting the pupil.
—Ralph Waldo Emerson

Here's a list of some historically prominent self-taught students. Do any of these names ring a bell?

- Leonardo da Vinci
- Abe Lincoln
- Malcolm X
- Benjamin Franklin
- Charles Darwin
- the Wright Brothers
- Herman Melville
- Ernest Hemingway
- Ray Bradbury
- Thomas Edison

All are considered *autodidacts*, those who are either partially or completely self-taught. Many overcame overwhelming odds to do this. They were able to achieve great things by believing in their own abilities.

Keith Moon is widely considered one of the greatest drummers of all time. He had just three lessons. Jimi Hendrix is considered one of the most influential electric guitarists in the history of music. He learned to play by ear. David Bowie had only a few singing lessons and taught himself to play five instruments. Rap superstar Eminem dropped out of high school at age seventeen. His love of words comes from a love of reading, and he has even read the dictionary front to back several times. Steven Spielberg was rejected from film school and dropped out of college. He didn't earn his degree until 2002.

In the School of Thought, you are both teacher and student. It's time to test your mettle, but don't worry. Acing this test is simple. It all starts with self-respect.

Go to the head of the class.

93

Meditation

• •

Sometimes I suffer from indigestion of the mind.
—Carrie Latet

How do you spell *relief*? *M-e-d-i-t-a-t-i-o-n*.

It is estimated that we have 70,000 thoughts per day. Since there are 86,400 seconds in a day, that means we have nearly one thought per second. It's exhausting just to think about—oops, there goes another thought!

When you've had one-too-many helpings of food for thought and your brain is stuffed, the best way to clean your plate is through meditation. A mere twenty minutes of meditation a day reaps numerous physical and mental benefits—from weight loss to curing insomnia—and there are no side effects. This mental floss eliminates all those thoughts you've been gnawing on and those that have been eating at you.

If your mind is all talk, it's time to take the action of inaction. What do you need to start? Nothing—and the more of it, the better. No technology needed, no batteries required. Then what? Sit. Stay.

It's all a matter of mind over chatter.

94

Temptation

∙ ∙

Lead me not into temptation; I can find the way myself.

—Rita Mae Brown

The first lesson in resisting temptation? Never do anything you wouldn't want published on the front page of the daily news—or to explain to the paramedics!

When we think about temptation, the heavy hitters usually come to mind: the steamy extramarital affair, the sordid acts of embezzlement by an executive gone wrong. Temptation, however, is a daily affair. It comes in the form of the Girl Scout cookies coaxing you away from counting calories. It calls to you from your cell phone, urging you to text while driving—just this once. And it pushes you to put your two cents into a disagreement when it doesn't make sense to do so.

Our best defense in this temptation-filled world may be to watch how we label ourselves. Saying things like "I just can't resist sweets" or "Money always burns a hole in my pocket" only opens the door for pastries to parade in and cash to clear out.

Make a new name for yourself. Get rid of outdated labels like *Weak* and *Spineless*. Your updated alias? *Self-Control*. Next time temptation whispers in your ear, don't answer.

Be a name-dropper.

95

Self-Love

• •

> If you can't see anything beautiful about yourself, get
> a better mirror.
>
> —Shane Kocyzan

Mirror, mirror on the wall . . . perception need an overhaul? Let's reflect.

Are you hyper-focused on the physical—seeing only wrinkles and crow's-feet instead of crinkles and laugh lines from a lifetime of smiles? Do you see a balding head instead of more face to love?

The one sure thing about time is that it passes. Defining ourselves solely by our appearance spells trouble with a capital *T-i-m-e*. Embrace the art of aging gracefully without disgrace. Not one of us is getting any younger. We're all on the clock.

Take a long, hard look at how you view yourself. Look past the superficial. Your inner beauty has nothing to do with bulging biceps or six-pack abs. It doesn't go away if your waistline expands or your hair turns gray. Strive to see the timeless you, even if you need reading glasses. And a better mirror.

Who's the fairest of them all?

96

Self-Fulfilling Prophecy

• •

> I always wanted to be somebody, but now I realize I
> should have been more specific.
>
> —Lily Tomlin

Believe it or not, you are a prophet, and your future
lies in your own very capable hands.

It's all a matter of mind over matter. When you believe
in yourself, your behavior reflects confidence, and you
manifest the very conditions necessary for success.
Mind-boggling!

But it's no laughing matter when your prophecies
aren't profitable. Then you create circumstances that
reinforce negative or false beliefs. Statements like "I've
always been the black sheep in my family" or "Things
just never go my way" have as much power to shape
your future as those that come from a place of faith,
fortitude, and fearlessness.

Are you a non-prophet—not daring to dream,
believing that you are powerless over what life hands
you? Are you the prophet of doom or the prophet of

whom you intend to become? Never mind what has come before. Starting now, take matters into your own hands and design your destiny. There's no better person for the job.

Mind your matters.

97

Envy

· ·

"Normal is an illusion. What is normal for the spider
is chaos for the fly."

—Morticia Adams

It's all smoke and mirrors, folks.

At any given moment, we might be suffering from
confusions, delusions, or illusions—maybe even all
three. We further deceive ourselves by imagining that
no one else is experiencing any of these hardships.
This self-deception leads us to falsely conclude that
we are surrounded by vibrantly healthy people with
dream jobs, perfect relationships, angelic children—all
of whom easily afford tropical vacations, sleek new
sports cars, granite countertops, and stainless-steel
appliances.

Some of us could win Academy Awards for masking
our personal struggles better than others, having
perfected the tricks of the masquerade trade. Though
we all have the faces we wear in public, when the
lights go down on the daily show, the masks come

off. There is not one among us who can escape the human condition.

Plato said, "Be kind, for everyone you meet is fighting a great battle." None of us wants pain—divorce, loss of a job, illness. We all want pleasure—a warm home filled with love and laughter, meaningful employment, good health. The only real illusion is that we have convinced ourselves that we are different.

Let's act like we're all in this together.

Support your supporting cast.

Self-Respect

• •

> Value yourself. The only people who appreciate a doormat are people with dirty shoes.
>
> —Leo Buscaglia

Feeling like a human doormat? As long as you're lying down, you'll get stepped on.

While it's important to play well with others, there are times when you need to draw a line in the sandbox. Bullies come in all shapes, sizes, and ages, too. They're not happy until they push you in the mud and take your toys—right along with your pride.

Playing it safe might mean playing by someone else's rules, ones that aren't necessarily right for you. Love yourself enough to speak up. Respect yourself enough to reclaim your power. Silence may be golden, but what good is a voice if you're afraid to use it? No one can take your dignity unless you surrender it.

It's time to level the playing field, and you can't do that from ground level. Get up. Capture the flag instead of waving the white one.

More power to you!

Anger

. . . .

> I don't have pet peeves like some people. I have whole kennels of irritation.
>
> —Whoopi Goldberg

If you're dog-tired of everyone yanking your chain, read on. Maybe you need to learn to keep your temper on a shorter leash.

Picture this: You are behind a slow driver who keeps tapping the breaks and checking road signs. Do you immediately begin to tailgate, intending for this unknown driver to sense your rage as you bear down at a menacingly close range? Do you curse about his or her inability to drive? Do you then lay on the horn?

Stop grinding your teeth and unclench your fists. When you're constantly aggravated by little annoyances, your body produces too much adrenaline. Over time, this leads to a weakened heart and stiffening arteries, and can triple your risk of heart attack. Scientists believe that chronic anger may be more dangerous than smoking and obesity as a factor that will contribute to an early death.

There's nothing warm and fuzzy about pet peeves that can kill you. Next time you're following an irritatingly slow driver, take a deep breath and count to ten. Since our neurological response to anger only lasts about two seconds, the extra eight seconds should help. Now consider this: Maybe this driver is new in town. Perhaps he's lost. But one thing is for sure—your anger is not shortening the other guy's life.

Call off the dogs before the fur flies. Learn to tame the savage beast.

Don't let 'em rattle your cage.

100

Animal Wisdom

. . . .

Wag more, bark less.
—Seen on a bumper sticker

We could all take a lesson from our dogs. Wagging more and barking less could help to create happier days not only for ourselves but for those around us.

Does your dog ever get stressed out because it's Monday? Or become moody and offended because the neighbor didn't smile and wave one particular morning? When was the last time your dog was dissatisfied with the size of his thighs? Has your dog recently seemed discouraged about the economy?

Bob Schieffer of CBS News once aired a short piece called "Lessons Learned from Man's Best Friend." Here are the talking points, the simple things we can learn when dogs become our teachers.

1. Always run to greet loved ones when they come home.
2. Never pass the opportunity to go for a joy ride.

3. Recognize the ecstasy of fresh air and wind in your face.
4. Take naps.
5. Stretch before rising.
6. Run, romp, and play daily.
7. Thrive on attention and let people touch you.
8. Avoid biting when a simple growl will do.
9. On warm days, lie on your back in the grass.
10. On hot days, drink lots of water and find the shade.
11. When you're happy, dance around and wag your entire body.
12. Enjoy long walks.
13. Be loyal.
14. Never pretend to be something you're not.
15. If what you want is buried, dig deep until you find it.
16. When someone is having a bad day, be silent, sit close by, and nuzzle them gently.

We'd be better off, better people . . . if we acted more like dogs.

Doggone it!

CPSIA information can be obtained
at www.ICGtesting.com
Printed in the USA
JSHW022032151222
34911JS00002B/10